T0129634

THE PRACTICAL STRATEGIES SERIES
IN GIFTED EDUCATION

series editors
FRANCES A. KARNES & KRISTEN R. STEPHENS

Advanced Placement Programs and Gifted Students

Elissa F. Brown, Ph.D.

Routledge
Taylor & Francis Group
NEW YORK AND LONDON

First published 2010 by Prufrock Press Inc.

Published 2021 by Routledge
605 Third Avenue, New York, NY 10017
2 Park Square, Milton Park, Abingdon, Oxon OX14 4RN

Routledge is an imprint of the Taylor & Francis Group, an informa business

ISBN 13: 978-1-59363-378-3 (pbk)

Contents

Series Preface

The Practical Strategies Series in Gifted Education offers teachers, counselors, administrators, parents, and other interested parties up-to-date instructional techniques and information on a variety of issues pertinent to the field of gifted education. Each guide addresses a focused topic and is written by an individual with authority on the issue. Several guides have been published. Among the titles are:

- *Acceleration Strategies for Teaching Gifted Learners*
- *Curriculum Compacting: An Easy Start to Differentiating for High-Potential Students*
- *Enrichment Opportunities for Gifted Learners*
- *Independent Study for Gifted Learners*
- *Motivating Gifted Learners*
- *Questioning Strategies for Teaching the Gifted*
- *Social & Emotional Teaching Strategies*
- *Using Media & Technology with Gifted Students*

For a current listing of available guides within the series, please contact Prufrock Press at 800-998-2208 or visit http://www.prufrock.com.

The predominant service delivery option for secondary gifted students in America's high schools for the past two decades has been Advanced Placement (AP) and International Baccalaureate (IB) programs (Callahan, 2003). The AP program was developed by the College Board in the mid-1950s and was never intended to be specifically for gifted students. At its inception, the AP program enrolled about 1,200 students; however, today the program boasts more than 1 million students. Similarly, the IB program, introduced in the early 1970s, enrolls more than 30,000 students nationwide (International Baccalaureate North America, 2004). For thousands of students, the courses associated with these two programs represent the first time in which they feel academically challenged, are taught by teachers with great depth of content knowledge, and are in an enriching and comfortable learning environment. Students do not have to be formally identified as gifted to enroll in either AP or IB courses; however, some schools or school systems do establish criteria to determine student readiness for participating in these courses. Table 1 provides the purpose and criteria for eligibility for both the AP and IB programs.

Table 1

Purpose and Criteria for Advanced Placement and
International Baccalaureate

Program	Purpose	Criteria for Eligibility
Advanced Placement	To provide high-achieving and self-motivated students opportunities to enroll in advanced courses of study and have the opportunity to earn college credit and/or advanced placement while enrolled in high school.	Eligibility is determined by Preliminary Scholastic Aptitude Test (PSAT) scores and student's readiness to engage in postsecondary level work as indicated by subject-area teacher and previous performance.
International Baccalaureate	To provide an advanced level of high school coursework designed to meet various international university entrance standards. To provide highly motivated students from diverse linguistic, cultural, and educational backgrounds with the intellectual, social, and critical perspectives needed to excel in college and beyond.	Student must: • be enrolled in a school authorized by the International Baccalaureate Association (IBO), and • demonstrate high level of achievement or preparation at the middle school and pre-IB levels.

The focus of this volume will be on the Advanced Placement program. It will address misconceptions about AP courses, the benefits of AP courses for gifted learners, suggested core and targeted teaching strategies for differentiation within AP courses, and supporting and impeding structures for implementing and sustaining a coherent AP program within a high school program of studies.

The AP program is intended to provide high school students with advanced content at the same level as an introductory college course. A typical introductory college course emphasizes breadth of content over depth because it is designed as a survey course, with the assumption being that students who wish to pursue a specialized domain within the content area will explore depth of content in upper level college courses, usually in their third or fourth year.

Mattimore (2009) cites four myths about AP courses:

- *AP courses are about memorization and do not require students to think critically.* Although AP exams do require students to understand basic facts within a particular area, students are expected to build upon this knowledge by making inferences, drawing conclusions, and analyzing patterns.
- *High school teachers lack expertise to teach college-level classes.* AP teachers are encouraged to receive specialized training though the College Board. The College Board offers hundreds of workshops each year for this purpose. In addition, teachers have access to college textbooks, man-

uals, test banks, and other resources that are similar to those provided to college professors.

- *Awarding college credit reduces chances for wider intellectual exploration in college.* On the contrary, AP courses allow students to bypass introductory courses that are sometimes required prerequisites and help broaden the college experience by giving students additional opportunities to delve further into a subject or pursue a double major.
- *College courses provide greater intellectual breadth and depth than AP courses.* Introductory college courses are typically lecture classes (sometimes large) where students have limited personal contact with the instructor. Sometimes a graduate student teaches these courses. AP high school courses are typically small, more personalized, and taught by a highly qualified AP teacher. Mattimore (2009) does encourage the College Board and colleges and universities to monitor AP classes to ensure that coursework is equivalent to college-level work.

Although the College Board does not set entrance criteria for students to enroll in AP courses, many schools have informally operationalized a system in which AP courses are only for identified gifted students. This additional misconception has the unintended consequence of undermining this valuable educational opportunity for all students.

Student Perceptions

Students have expressed mixed reactions to AP courses. Hertberg-Davis and Callahan (2008) conducted interviews with 200 students from 23 high schools about their perceptions of AP courses and IB programs. In terms of being academically challenged, although these students reported they felt the coursework made them "think critically" (Hertberg-Davis & Callahan, 2008, p. 202), they complained about the quantity of work and the sacrifices they made (e.g., less time for work or social life) in order to keep up with the workload. Secondly, students cited that the teachers were skilled, knowledgeable, and caring. Statements such as, "I think they are some of the best teachers I've ever had" (Hertberg-Davis & Callahan, 2008, p. 203) were typical. Lastly, students indicated they preferred the learning environment, primarily because they were surrounded by other students of similar motivation and ability.

Overall, students indicated that although there were drawbacks to AP and IB courses, the long-term benefits outweighed short-term frustrations. VanTassel-Baska (2008) noted:

> AP courses remain a strong option for gifted students. AP is not a magic bullet at the secondary level, but it offers a very strong option for gifted students to receive college credit and move forward in a compressed time model. The quality of the courses is important to that capacity to move flexibly forward in a student's area of strength. (p. 1)

Despite the many successes and benefits cited by students and some perceived myths, unresolved problems pervade the implementation of Advanced Placement programs in schools. Many of the students interviewed in the Hertberg-Davis and Callahan (2008) study felt the coursework and environment were too rigid. Others cited lack of prerequisite knowledge as a barrier to success. A third concern is for deep implementation of AP course syllabi by trained teachers. Schools must make sure that instruction is producing real learning as judged by student performance. Where this is not occurring, improvements need to be made. Finally, access to Advanced Placement for all students is of concern. There is a need to ensure that all students who could profit from AP are enrolled. Special outreach efforts to economically disadvantaged and minority students are critical to make certain these students are appropriately represented in such programs.

Benefits of AP Courses for Gifted Learners

There are several benefits when considering why gifted secondary students should participate in AP courses. First, the underlying premise in the coursework is accelerated content, which by most accounts matches the rate of development for gifted students. Not only do these students acquire more information in a shorter amount of time, but they think with the depth and insight of older students. Research on the benefits of acceleration for gifted students include:

- improved motivation, scholarship, and confidence of gifted and talented students over time;
- prevention of habits of mental laziness;
- earlier access to and completion of more advanced opportunities; and
- reduction of the total cost of college education and time toward a degree and professional preparation (Colangelo, Assouline, & Gross, 2004).

Second, AP courses afford students the opportunity to engage in college-level work while still in high school. Thus, success in these courses sends the message to colleges and universities that a student is ready and has the prerequisite knowledge for placement in college courses.

Third, AP courses are designed by a team of college professors, experts in relative fields, and secondary school teachers. Courses are reviewed and revised annually, thus students acquire the up-to-date core knowledge used by professionals and the authentic tools to inquire about how knowledge is generated in a given field.

Fourth, AP coursework typically emphasizes advanced concepts. Current research has suggested that focusing student learning on major ideas in a discipline can both help retention and provide a mental framework on which students can build their understanding as new applications are made (VanTassel-Baska, 1998).

Fifth, at the culmination of coursework, students typically take an exam that may earn them college credit or advanced college placement. Most of the colleges and universities in the United States and in more than 40 countries grant students credit, placement, or both for qualifying exam grades. Implications for being awarded credit or skipping introductory courses and entering higher level courses (e.g., placement) are financial savings, the opportunity to take additional coursework in college, early graduation, the ability to pursue a double major or a combined degree, and time to study and travel abroad.

Sixth, AP courses are often given additional "weight" in high school when determining culminating grade point averages (GPA). These weighted grades can affect a student's class rank upon graduation, thus making him or her a more desirable candidate for highly selective colleges and universities.

Seventh, students report that AP courses provide the challenge, quality of instruction, and learning environment that meet their academic and intellectual needs (Hertberg-Davis & Callahan, 2008).

Finally, AP, through the rigor of its course structure, provides a major emphasis on critical thinking. Teaching critical thinking requires domain-specific tactics and the development of a strong knowledge base. In addition, much of the AP material in most subject areas is performance-based, requiring students to exhibit analytical, interpretative, synthesis, and evaluative skills to perform the task demands at high levels of accomplishment.

Even though there are benefits for gifted students to take AP courses, Gallagher (2009) contended that an overemphasis on the tangible reward (access to college credit) sends a troubling message to students and faculty. Instead, the experience, exploration, awareness, discovery, and creativity developed through participation in AP courses should receive the most focus.

The substance of gifted education as a field rests on the faithful application of curriculum and instructional approaches that are designed to serve gifted students in schools and other contexts. Consequently, the importance of the influence of these approaches cannot be overestimated as systematic differentiation in the field is nested in teacher understanding of how to translate curriculum and instruction in appropriate ways and with diverse gifted populations. If we assume, therefore, that gifted secondary students will continue enrolling in AP courses, then within those classrooms, what types of differentiation in curricula and instructional practices should be employed to ensure that a variety of needs are met? Are there key strategies that teachers should use when teaching AP coursework to students? The following section will explore these considerations.

Core Teaching Strategies

Even though AP is widely implemented in high schools, research on differentiation within the various courses is limited. Little research has been done to document the degree to which AP courses are differentiated to meet the myriad of student needs. Consider the following scenario:

> As a high school AP World History teacher, Margo teaches one 90-minute block of world history. The chronological scope of this is from 8000 B.C.E. to the present, with the period of 8000 B.C.E. to 600 C.E. serving as the foundation for the balance of the course. Additionally, the course spans global coverage with Africa, the Americas, Asia, Europe, and Oceania all represented. Many of the students have little or no prior knowledge of the material, although some gifted students have extensive knowledge of given topics. Given the time-consuming and complex task of covering the material to meet course goals and objectives, how does

Margo adapt the curriculum and differentiate instruction to challenge all learners, even the gifted ones?

This teacher could benefit from implementing a few core and targeted teaching strategies that would enable content coverage as well as foster student engagement. There are some core approaches that can be employed across all AP subjects that have been effective in working with gifted learners. They represent a set of strategies that can be implemented in any secondary grade level across disciplines. These sample core strategies provide the teacher and student with valuable evidence of general understanding. Six suggested core strategies are described below.

Core Strategy #1: Preassessment and Diagnostic Follow-Up

The use of old tests at the beginning of the year, especially in subjects that are most clearly sequential in learning such as English or history, can be useful in ascertaining the level of functioning of each student in the class, so that more tailored instruction might follow. The use of preassessments at targeted points in the semester or year allows students to demonstrate prerequisite knowledge in a specific area. The key to implementing preassessment though, is the degree to which a teacher uses the resulting data to modify future content and instruction. Just using a preassessment with no follow-up is an inefficient use of time and defeats the purpose.

Core Strategy #2: In-Class Power Tasks

Use of timed, performance-based tasks to stimulate interest and monitor readiness for a novel task is an important instructional approach to employ. Immediate feedback through oral discussion along with individual assessment of performance heightens the opportunity for authentic learning to occur. For example, having students write a persuasive essay in response to a prompt within a time frame teaches students to be succinct, cogent, and comprehensive in their writing.

Core Strategy #3: Specific Feedback for Improvement

Students need advice, counsel, and tutoring on how to move up and improve their assessment scores (i.e., from a 3 to a 4). Coaching may be required in order to encourage such progress. Peer or teacher feedback can be beneficial for students to target specific areas for improvement.

Core Strategy #4: Targeted Homework

The principle that may apply here is "less is more." The tendency of teachers, because of the need to cover extensive material, may be to pile on homework to an extent beyond what students would typically receive in a college class. A better strategy is well-selected homework within the reach of the students' ability to complete in a reasonable amount of time. Difficult problems and analyses should be done in class with easier applications and analysis out of class.

Core Strategy #5: Tutorial Review and Test Practice

Providing review sessions beginning at least 6 weeks prior to exams is a strong incentive to high student performance. Old tests should be distributed and used liberally in preparation. Research has consistently shown the highest effect sizes (2.00) for such tutorial approaches (Bloom, 1984).

Core Strategy #6: Taking the AP Exam

In general, students should be encouraged to take the AP exam if they have taken the AP course and are passing it. The exam itself constitutes a learning experience. Score results should always be viewed in light of preassessment data, with a clear eye to evidencing improvement.

The employment of these core strategies should not only lead to stronger student performance on the AP exams, but also to greater teacher satisfaction with course instruction, as the teaching-learning dynamic becomes more palpable in the classroom.

Targeted Strategies

Targeted teaching strategies are those that help students develop the ability to make informed and reasoned decisions. Furthermore, such reasoning ability is achieved not by memorizing a series of facts in a textbook, but by developing the habits of mind utilized by professionals in disciplines of study. Developing habits of mind in our students requires teachers to teach complexity through active learning and critical inquiry. Even a basic geography lesson on maps can have students question why a map is drawn a certain way or what the map reveals about the point of view of the cartographer rather than merely accepting the map at face value. Such habits of mind can be developed through specific strategies that teachers can employ.

Targeted teaching strategies are those that allow for additional depth, complexity, and rigor within a content area. These strategies aid students in developing expertise and the habits of mind of a professional. There are research-based strategies that are effective with all learners, and in particular gifted learners, and can be adapted and implemented in any AP course. The following four targeted strategies merely represent a small sample of the many strategies available to teachers.

Targeted Strategy #1: Reasoning Through a Situation or Event

Reasoning through a situation or event (see Figure 1) is an application of Paul's (1992) Elements of Reasoning that helps students to identify different points of view or perspectives relative to a given event or situation and then evaluate the assumptions and implications of diverse positions. Based on the elements and premise of the Paul model, this reasoning model should be used when analyzing a specific event where two or more people or groups of people conflict with one another and have a vested interest in the outcome of the event. This model or approach can be used across curricular areas to allow students to focus on the complexity of issues, whether in the social sciences or humanities.

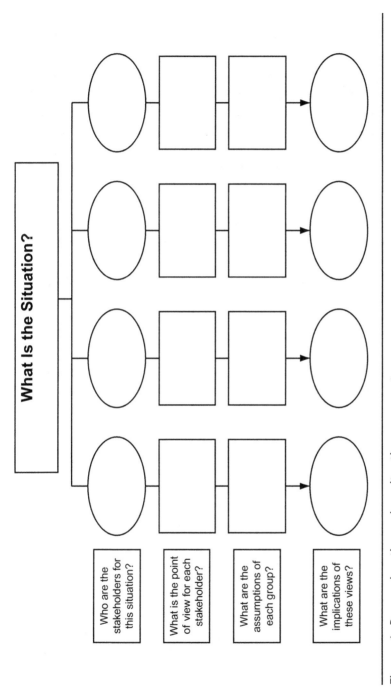

Figure 1. Reasoning through a situation or event.

Note. Reprinted with permission of the Center for Gifted Education, The College of William and Mary.

A student identifies the purpose or issue to be explored at the top of the model. An issue implies multiple perspectives and is controversial. It is ambiguous and as information or research is gathered, the problem or issue may change. Another important feature of an issue is that it is personally relevant. A group of people care about the issue and are willing to spend time resolving it or proposing a resolution to the problem. Teachers need to be mindful that students identify an issue that allows for a variety of points of view.

The second step in the model is to identify stakeholder groups. These are groups of individuals who would have a particular perspective on the relevant issue. Once a stakeholder group is identified, then students work vertically in the model analyzing potential assumptions and implications by a particular stakeholder group. This model can be used prior to a class debate, or students can be divided to assume a particular stakeholder lens and conduct further research. This process provides an objective and structured way to view an issue through a variety of points of view. Understanding the assumptions and implications of a particular stakeholder group infuses habits of mind, complexity, and personal relevance on any particular issue. Teachers can facilitate a discussion by posing follow-up questions. For example:

- What are the implications of the interactions of the various assumptions?
- What has caused these different points of view to develop?
- What are potential conflicts that can result from this situation or issue?
- What are possible resolutions for this situation or issue?
- How do society's values or a given culture's values influence the assumptions and implications of a particular stakeholder group?

Targeted Strategy #2: Analyzing Primary Sources

The Analyzing Primary Sources model (Center for Gifted Education, 2000) allows students to confront a historical document, generate questions to ask of it, and critically examine information garnered from the source. The chart depicted in Figure

Analyzing Primary Sources

Document Title: _____

A: Establishing a context and intent for the source:
- Author:
- Time/when was it written
- Briefly describe the culture of the time and list related events of the time
- Purpose (Why was the document created?)
- Audience (Who was the document created for?)

B. Understanding the source:
- What problems/issues/events does the source address?
- What are the main points/ideas/arguments?
- What assumptions/values/feelings does the author reflect?
- What actions/outcomes does the author expect? From whom?

C. Evaluating/Interpreting the source:
- Authenticity/Reliability (Could the source be invented, edited, or mistranslated? What corroborating evidence do you have about the source? Does the author know enough about the topic to discuss it?)
- Representative (How typical is the source of others of the same period? What other information might you need to find this out?)
- What could the consequences of this document be? (What would happen if the author's plan were carried out? What could happen to the author when people read this? How might this document affect or change public opinions?)
- What were the actual consequences? What really happened as a result of this document?
- Short-term/long term: What new or different interpretation does this source provide about the historical period?

Figure 2. Analyzing primary sources model.

Note. Reprinted with permission of the Center for Gifted Education, The College of William and Mary.

2 guides students from establishing a context and purpose for the source to evaluating and interpreting the source, including its authenticity/reliability and consequences/outcomes.

There are many ways to use the Analyzing Primary Sources model: individually or in small or large groups. The model can be used during a lesson to deepen the understanding of a particular source or at the end of a lesson as an authentic assessment. It can be used to compare and contrast two primary source documents of similar time periods or those produced by the same author(s). Much of the content employed in AP courses comes from primary source documents. This template provides a schema and structure for students when they are considering primary sources.

Targeted Strategy #3: Developing Research Skills

Having gifted students engaged in research provides an authentic learning experience that can be tailored to their particular learning needs and predilections. It provides an opportunity for students to acquire a deep understanding of a particular issue or topic and cultivate competence in research by challenging assumptions, establishing a knowledge base in an area or discipline, and developing specific research skills. Research is inquiry-based and allows for a high degree of autonomous learning. There are many research models available to teachers to incorporate in the classroom. Figure 3 outlines the seven major steps in conducting research as an ongoing, continuous cycle that teachers should strive to develop in students.

The first step in the research process is for students to identify an issue or topic of interest. Although the issue or topic may be determined somewhat by the AP content, it should be linked to a student's interest, as well. Conducting research in an area that is personally relevant to the student makes the entire project meaningful and maintains student engagement.

The second step involves developing a strong knowledge base. This step is prior to generating questions or problems to be solved because reading and learning about a particular subject or issue allows students to identify gaps and trends, formulate research hypotheses, and verify the credibility of sources. During this step, students consider different formats for relevant sources and the types of information that can be gleaned from a particular resource. For example, interviewing an individual provides a primary source, but one where acquired information is perceptual and biased, having been shaped by the personal experiences of the individual. In contrast, gathering information from a peer-reviewed article provides data but may lose the personal insight.

During the third step in the research process, students generate and formulate questions based on deep knowledge of a partic-

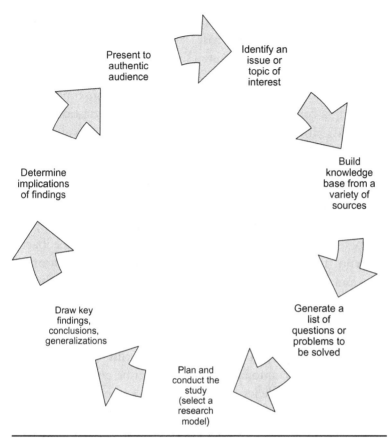

Figure 3. The research process.

ular area. The next step (step four) focuses on planning the study. One key component of this step is to select the most appropriate research methods (e.g., historical research, descriptive research, or experimental research). Having a written research plan provides structure for student researchers, so students should be encouraged to document the process.

Students isolate key findings, trends, generalizations, and draw conclusions during step five of the research process. Conclusions may include modifying or developing a new theory, creating a model for clarification, making recommendations for future study based on trends or data, or drawing conclusions based on a threshold of responses across data sources.

From these conclusions, step six has students determine the implications of their findings. Questions considered during this step include: What are the positive or negative consequences of following a certain conclusion? Are there new questions to be answered? How do the findings or recommendations affect different stakeholder groups?

Lastly, students need to present their research to an authentic audience, preferably one that has a vested interest in the topic or issue of study. This provides a venue for feedback and verification from professionals in the field. It also affords students an opportunity to reflect on their work based on constructive feedback. Students must, in presenting, be cogent in their articulation of ideas and succinct in what they want to share. Finally, it should be noted that the entire process is cyclical, encouraging students to engage in research again.

Targeted Strategy #4: Targeted Thinking Skills

Another instructional process that can be employed across AP courses and grade levels is the strategic embedding of thinking skills at the beginning, middle, and end of each lesson to ensure analytical reasoning and problem solving are taking place throughout a unit of study.

There are several strategies that teachers might consider for embedding thinking skills for the gifted into content areas. One way to approach which thinking strategy to implement is to consider the relevant mental processes used by a given area of study. In literature, for example, one might engage in the following mental processes:
- interpreting and creating analogies,
- using deductive and inductive reasoning,
- making inferences,
- discerning authors' purpose or point of view, and
- evaluating arguments.

Thinking skills in mathematics might be viewed a little differently. Mental processes typically employed in mathematics might include:

- looking for patterns, systems, and logical inferences;
- guessing and testing;
- making a model;
- working backward;
- setting up an equation; and
- mathematical modeling based on assumptions.

In science, students should be engaged in scientific processes. The thinking model here might include:

- selecting a problem or issue,
- studying the problem,
- making hypotheses,
- collecting data,
- analyzing and interpreting data,
- drawing conclusions and testing their relevance to the problem,
- making implications, and
- replicating, as necessary.

As these examples suggest, implementing thinking skills into content areas will vary by discipline and by the nature of the required objectives. One challenge is to define and clarify the type of thinking ahead of time and to work through a series of thinking strategies deliberately in order for students' thinking to be complex, provocative, and to become more sophisticated over time. The inclusion of thinking skills is predicated on the following key assumptions:

- Thinking is a complex process, made up of many skills.
- Thinking is dependent upon student discourse to relay understanding and allow for improvement.
- Thinking is integrated and interrelated with application.

- Thinking involves the development of an inquiring mind as well as mastery of the skills and processes of a discipline.
- Thinking is best taught within the context of content.

There is little evidence of the effectiveness of specific thinking skills programs (Sternberg & Lubart, 1993), but evidence does suggest that teaching thinking as procedural knowledge to be internalized can promote advanced learning (Marzano, 1993).

Summary

If we revisit the AP World History teacher scenario, Margo could select a targeted strategy such as the research model by assigning different time spans but allowing students to choose the topic or issue to be studied. This would enable her to cover a large amount of material while strengthening research skills in students. Margo also could employ a core strategy such as preassessment for a particular skill (e.g., map skills) and, based on the results of the preassessment, shorten the amount of time spent on that particular skill.

Students should be engaged in core strategies for covering the material and being prepared in an AP course, but they also should be frequently engaged in targeted strategies that encourage reasoning, research, thinking, and understanding points of view. By employing both core and targeted teaching strategies, teachers of AP courses can be assured that their students are benefitting from research-based strategies that promote differentiation and depth within any AP course.

Students representing 16,464 secondary schools took AP exams in 2007 (College Board, 2008), but providing a coherent AP program in high schools encompasses other components than just offering courses and their concomitant exam. The range and scope of AP courses may vary, as well as the policies and practices around which students take the exam. AP courses require a commitment of resources and capacity of personnel, but sometimes that falls short in terms of sustained growth and program articulation. If a school wants an effective, well-articulated, comprehensive, and coherent AP program (not just a list of AP courses), considerations need to be given to those supporting or impeding structures for implementing and sustaining a coherent AP program as an integrated part of the overall high school program of studies. Table 2 displays the supporting and impeding structures for implementing high-powered, research-based curriculum and instructional practices in AP courses.

Table 2

Supporting and Impeding Structures for Implementing High-Powered Curriculum and Instructional Practices in AP Courses

Components	Supporting Structures	Impeding Structures
Professional Development	Strong professional development program with sustained renewal opportunities. Strategic decisions are made about professional development aligned with school improvement goals.	Eclectic approach to professional development. Sending new hires for AP training with limited support, conversation, or follow-up.
Fiscal Allocation and Support	Fiscal support for curriculum, support materials, and professional development to ensure fidelity of implementation.	Fiscal support for only professional development without support materials or support materials without professional development lacks coherency.
Leadership	School and central office provide strong leadership to support the concept of higher expectations for all students. Leadership supports implementation of advanced curriculum.	School and central office focus on remediation and those below proficiency without attending to higher level courses.
Accountability	AP exams have demonstrated accountability for learning and strong connections to higher education.	Preparation for state testing mania has led many administrators and teachers to focus on state values to the exclusion of other measures of assessment.
Access	Targeted and proactive measures are taken to ensure that a diverse body of students enrolls in and completes AP courses.	School policies, grading practices, and requirements of prerequisites limit opportunities for ensuring all students have access to high-end learning.

Supporting Structures

Supporting structures for implementing a coherent AP program involve consideration to the following areas: professional development, fiscal allocation resources, leadership, accountability, and access.

Professional Development

Both teachers and administrators need strong professional development for supporting implementation efforts. Professional development has been emphasized as a key component in recent national educational agendas (e.g., No Child Left Behind Act; NCLB, 2001) and continues to be viewed as the primary mechanism by which teachers update their skills in order to implement curriculum and school reform initiatives.

School and district administrators should receive professional development sessions on curriculum implementation not so much targeted at pedagogical practices but rather at issues that may result from teachers implementing curriculum that extends beyond state-level curriculum frameworks. Teachers should receive training on the teaching and learning models, performance-based assessment approaches, and resources that can extend, enrich, and augment implementation efforts. Frequently, teachers of AP courses only receive training linked to a specific course and the exam. Such training is typically not embedded within a larger context of a high school program of studies. Lastly, both teachers and administrators should receive training on ways to advocate for meaningful curriculum and AP programs to parents, other educators (e.g., school counselors), and school board members.

Fiscal Allocation and Resources

The use of fiscal resources to purchase materials for teachers and students in terms of the curriculum units and associated support materials such as novels, science kits, and primary source documents is another supporting structure that enriches the AP program. Professional development without proper material support is like providing a house with no utilities, furniture, or food. Additional resources should be set aside to allow for continuous purchasing of materials and exams, as well as follow-up technical assistance opportunities.

Leadership

A third supporting structure is strong and effective leadership. Leadership in the classroom, at the school, and in the central office is important for implementing high-powered curriculum because teachers need to feel that their principals are not only instructional leaders but appreciate a rigorous curriculum in all of its manifestations. Central office support is critical to avoid isolation by the school or the teacher and to signal strong centralized support for implementing curriculum that is evidence-based. This type of leadership supports the literature on change being most effective and potentially institutionalized if support is bidirectional, given from the bottom-up (classroom level) and the top-down (school and district levels; Fullan, 2001).

Accountability

Another support structure is the use of accountability measures, both formative and summative, in order to inform teachers and administrators of student progress throughout the implementation of an AP course. Using additional assessment measures beyond the AP exam, such as performance-based tasks that are nested within units of study, allow teachers to make, if necessary, daily adjustments to their instructional practices. The use of core and targeted teaching strategies provide a diagnostic-prescriptive approach to implementing the curriculum while honoring students' talents. By embedding these approaches throughout the course, teachers can fully implement a comprehensive and differentiated approach.

Access

A final support structure in developing AP program coherency is ensuring that the courses, while remaining rigorous, are accessible to all students. Proactive measures should be taken at the school and district levels to ensure that the student body taking the courses reflects the larger demographics of the school and school system. Programs and policies designed to help students access and have greater success in college-level coursework should be in place. Efforts to expand the program are important, but not at the expense of student access. Educators and administrators have to work collaboratively to foster access to AP courses among low-income students and culturally diverse populations. This may mean that attention is paid to those courses preceding AP courses, grading practices and school policies about prerequisites, and that schools emphasize a stronger articulation of middle and high school education.

Impeding Structures

To ensure coherency in coursework, teacher preparation, and accessibility to students, administrators and teachers should be aware of the potential impeding structures or barriers that may prevent a thorough, comprehensive approach to AP program implementation.

Approaches to Professional Development

One barrier for implementing a coherent AP program is the eclectic approach to professional development and new hires. That is, when a current AP teacher retires or leaves the school, the typical response is to replace him or her with an equally qualified professional, send that individual to AP course training, and assume a high-quality course. Although this is applaudable, it is also problematic. Little attention is being paid to course-taking patterns within the school, ongoing needs for professional development, and how the AP program is aligned to school improvement plans.

Ongoing Fiscal Support

Another barrier to successful implementation of an AP program lies in the lack of targeted fiscal resources. Ongoing fiscal support for additional materials that enhance the offered curriculum is needed for fidelity of implementation. Beyond a one-time allotment, sustaining AP courses within the framework of a high school program of study requires deliberate use of resources and support.

Focus on Remediation

Finally, leadership, accountability, and lack of access to courses limit the scope of the program. Schools focusing on remediation and bringing students up to proficiency rather than on high-level courses and raising expectations for all students has made implementation of AP curriculum and instruction—whose hallmark is higher level thinking—very difficult. Administrators need to realize that all students can think at higher levels, but without the opportunity to do so will continue to underperform. Thus "skill and drill" approaches become the substitution for rich curriculum and instruction.

Conclusion

Although AP coursework may not be for every student, the program puts those students who choose it on a deliberate path toward the accrual of educational advantage in key areas of learning. AP programs are integral to secondary education, and because of early access to college credit, have incentivized a high school program of studies. For gifted students, integrating core and targeted strategies in AP courses ensures that exploration, discovery, creativity, and depth are embedded forms of instruction and that these courses are responsive to individual precocities. These strategies would not only honor the AP curriculum but respond to the nature of the student.

Resources

AP Central
http://apcentral.collegeboard.com/apc/Controller.jpf
Within the College Board's Web site, this site houses a multitude of resources for Advanced Placement teachers.

Center for Gifted Education at The College of William and Mary
http://www.cfge.wm.edu
This site offers differentiated curriculum units in relevant domains. Within each unit of study are research-based teaching models based on Joyce VanTassel-Baska's Integrated Curriculum Model. These teaching models can be employed within an AP unit of study to differentiate for gifted learners.

College Board
http://www.collegeboard.com
This is the organization that manages the Advanced Placement program. A vast amount of resources for teachers, parents, and students are available through this website.

Follett Educational Services, Inc.
http://www.fes.follett.com/brand_new_books/AP_
testPreparationMaterials.cfm
Follett offers a complete line of AP exam test preparation materials.

The 5th Annual AP Report to the Nation
http://professionals.collegeboard.com/profdownload/ap-report-
to-nation-2009.pdf
This is an online report that provides relevant data specific to
the AP program.

**The Toolbox Revisited: Paths to Degree Completion
From High School Through College**
http://www.ed.gov/rschstat/research/pubs/toolboxrevisit/
toolbox.pdf
This is a data essay that follows a nationally representative cohort
of students from high school into postsecondary education and
asks what aspects of their formal schooling contribute to com-
pleting a bachelor's degree.

References

Bloom, B. S. (1984). The 2 Sigma problem: The search for methods of group instruction as effective as one-on-one tutoring. *Educational Researcher, 13,* 4–16.

Callahan, C. M. (2003). *Advanced Placement and International Baccalaureate programs for talented students in American high schools: A focus on science and math* (Research Monograph No. 03276). Storrs: University of Connecticut, National Research Center on the Gifted and Talented.

Center for Gifted Education. (2000). *Teaching and learning models.* Williamsburg, VA: Author.

Colangelo, N., Assouline, S. G., & Gross, M. U. M. (2004). *A nation deceived: How schools hold back America's brightest students* (Vol. 1). Iowa City: The University of Iowa, The Connie Belin & Jacqueline N. Blank International Center for Gifted Education and Talent Development.

College Board. (2008). *The 4th annual AP report to the nation.* New York, NY: Author.

Fullan, M. (2001). *The new meaning of educational change* (3rd ed.). New York, NY: Teachers College Press.

Gallagher, S. (2009). Myth 19: Is Advanced Placement an adequate program for gifted students? *Gifted Child Quarterly, 53,* 286–287.

Hertberg-Davis, H., & Callahan, C. M. (2008). A narrow escape: Gifted students' perceptions of Advanced Placement and International Baccalaureate programs. *Gifted Child Quarterly, 52,* 199–216.

International Baccalaureate North America. (2004). *May 2004 data summary report: A profile of diploma program test takers.* New York, NY: Author.

Marzano, R. (1993). *Cultivating thinking in English and the language arts.* Urbana, IL: National Council of Teachers of English.

Mattimore, P. (2009). 5 fundamental misconceptions about AP courses. *Chronicle of Higher Education, 55*(22), A33

No Child Left Behind Act of 2001, Pub. L. No. 104-110, 115 Stat. 1425 (2001).

Paul, R. (1992). *Critical thinking: What every person needs to survive in a rapidly changing world.* Rohnert Park, CA: Foundation for Critical Thinking.

Sternberg, R., & Lubart, T. (1993). Creative giftedness: A multivariate investment approach. *Gifted Child Quarterly, 37,* 7–15.

VanTassel-Baska, J. (1998). *Excellence in educating gifted and talented learners.* Denver, CO: Love.

VanTassel-Baska, J. (2008). AP for gifted students still a good choice. *Duke Gifted Letter, 8*(4), 1–2.

About the Author

Elissa F. Brown, Ph.D., is Director of Secondary Projects at the North Carolina Department of Public Instruction where she is engaged in statewide reform efforts for middle and high schools. Prior to her work at the state department, she was the director of the Center for Gifted Education at The College of William & Mary. She serves on the board of directors for the North Carolina Association for Research in Education (NCARE). She is a published author in the field of gifted education, and she is the recipient of the National Association for Gifted Children's 2004 Early Leader award. She has coordinated state and national gifted conferences and keynotes widely on a variety of topics. She has three children and resides in Chapel Hill, NC.

Printed in the United States
by Baker & Taylor Publisher Services